SAVAGE ACRES

First published in 2025 by
The Dedalus Press
13 Moyclare Road
Baldoyle
Dublin D13 K1C2
Ireland

www.dedaluspress.com

ISBN 9781915629371 (paperback)
ISBN 9781915629364 (hardback)

Dedalus Press titles are available in Ireland
from Argosy Books (www.argosybooks.ie) and in the UK
from Inpress Books (www.inpressbooks.co.uk).

Cover photograph:
'Martha, Queen of the DPLIPHE,' by Pete Smyth,
From *Local* (Gallery of Photography, Ireland, 2019),
by kind permission of the photographer.

Dedalus Press receives financial assistance from
The Arts Council / An Chomhairle Ealaíon.

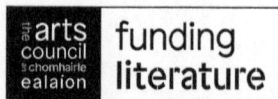

the arts council chomhairle ealaíon | funding literature

SAVAGE ACRES

KEITH PAYNE

DEDALUS PRESS

CONTENTS

PART 1

PART II

'A shiver now runs through the laurel hedge,
And washing flutters like the swaying lines
Of a new verse.'
—Ciaran Carson, 'The New Estate'

For Teo, who brought these poems with him.
And for Su, my first and fiercest reader.

PART 1

Twisted tassels scallop the blinds
The Green cambers even from this height
the reel of three hooded crows in flight.

No. 9: The Kitchen Island

No. 9 relishes the chance to marvel at his kitchen cabinets:
the soft-closing drawers, the toe-kick,
the red lacquer finish that shows his reflection
as he walks through the door

and sits to his very own kitchen island,
to a Wall's *Viennetta* ice-cream
that crackles as the cake-slice cleaves
the chocolate glacial layers.

But this is just the start of desserts to come.
There is a whole palette of sorbets,
an endless cascade of profiteroles and before too long
he'll be striding back from his shed
with crème brûlée in his head and a blow torch in his hand.

No. 7: The Sound of Things to Come

The idea of neighbours had never occurred to No. 7,
so every Sunday gave him the vapours
when that man from next door stood in his garden
and bringing his lips to the nipple
raised his alto sax in the air
and blew through *Beauty is a Rare Thing*.

The notes teased over the wall
insinuating themselves into his ears
as he stood galvanised by the kitchen sink
watching the sun clear the capstones of the shared back wall;
his fingers tapping on the tea towel
to *The Sound of Things to Come*.

No. 8: It's True What They Say

She wears her dressing gown round the house all day
and only when the sun goes down and the fire is alight

does she set the vinyl spinning, and with her dress just right
—her arms in place—

she twirls through the flickering on the walls
and dances with her shadow round the room.

No. 5: Thrust as He Might His Hands into His Cardigan Pockets

No. 5 cannot resist the strafe of children
he sees from his mullioned windows
    on a street full of mullioned windows.

Lifting the lid on the turntable, he slides the arm over the plate,
the needle picks up every abandoned hair and dust mote
crackles and spits   lifts the music into the room
and he listens with sympathy to the tympanum in the orchestra.

He slips out of his Argyle socks to the symphony's swell
as the tongue and groove ceiling opens to receive him
    and he is lifted into the mystic.

No. 2: Falling Slowly

"Yes, the newspapers were right:
snow was general all over Ireland."
—James Joyce, 'The Dead'

With her everyday so blue, No. 2 often escaped
down the lane at the bottom of the estate
where no mobile phone could triangulate her whereabouts
by the hedgerow where the crows squabbled in the snow.

>   And how many flakes fell that year
>   over all the roof slates,
>   over all the garden gates,
>   fell perfectly flawed on her tongue?

>   *Despite being made of ice*
>   *snow appears white in colour;*
>   *the diffuse reflection*
>   *of the whole spectrum of light.*

Tiny crystals expanding in the night
fall and accumulate, smothering the estate.

The catch of a horseshoe hung over a door
the scroll of the screen
the curving signature: *We've been*
but no one was home.

From the Shoulder of Mutton Estate I

With a mug of *Maxwell House*
he sits and watches the scraw he once brought home
grow into the lawn

till the morning he doesn't cross The Green
doesn't pay his fare and go upstairs
to his usual seat

but removes the roofing tacks from the shed
and sails the roofing felt
over the fence.

He winds the shower flex round the apple
tree and lays the bathroom taps on the grass
as if they'd all poured green;

you see he wants to return the plasterer's arc
spark the welder's torch
and burn the planners' maps

that insist on tarmacadam over all the savage acres.

No. 6: The Needle on the Scales

Loosening the hasps on her shoes
as the red kettle that shuddered all afternoon
is all of a sudden soundless

—the neighbours' everything and place mats,
carvery knives and cruet sets—

she kisses goodnight the photograph
and top of the stairs   into the bathroom
where she barely nudges the needle on the scales.

Children of the Reservation I: Marta

Marta, Queen of The Green,
black crow feathers hung from black plaits,
stands blanket-wrapped,
her face painted for war—or dance.

In From the Fields

the wind whirls down the *cul de sac*
where she leaves her door open
letting it play the wainscoting

The Fortune Teller

gave good counsel from her chambers
—a caravan down Fortunestown Lane—
took fortified wine in payment
that she'd use to catch pheasants
or share when the Councillor came,

who admired the roses pinking her wall,
the tangerines sat in the bowl,
who flushed to the flame that lit up his cheek
when she lifted the lid on her stove
and told him what he needed to know:

'A ribbon pinned to the reveal of a door
a pair of scissors in the palm of your hand
a motorway straight as the flight of a crow
tearing through the land,' and tipping an eye
she held his gaze with 'yes,
there will be a toll to pay.'

A hard-bristle brush sweeping the dross—
empty packet, crumpled, tossed.
The slide slumps in the playground.

Home to the Estate

'They didn't buckle easy back then,'
she says (bone shakers, the rattle just
right on the acoustic motorbike),
and off she pedals, humming along
to her own song high on her High Nellie.

Gis a backer, you might just drop us off?
We'll take the long road home, the metro-
nomic wobble as we round the curves
to the ranging music of the gears.

From the Shoulder of Mutton Estate II

Peeling back the architraves
we ran them through with a circular saw,

staked The Green into allotments
and with a lottery draw divided its quarter acre.

Corners surged with rhubarb
the compost heap gave its hot breath to the morning freeze.

Window reveals twirled with runner beans
and blooms foretold a harvest of artichoke hearts.

We renamed all the streets: now Crow,
Pancrocheen and Yellow Meadow fetched us home

to the Hedge School behind the oleaster
for courses on Sharpstone, Canterbury Spar and Thrown Dash;

all gravel, golden to the Shoulder of Mutton Estate
whose very foundations were coarse aggregate.

It All Hinges on This

Bicycle clips—
the serenity of freewheeling down the hill
through the concrete bollards,

through the new estate,
through the roundabout
and out to the sea salt air

for repair.

No. 11: Building a Home

There were nights she came home and the house was gone,
so hanging her coat on a branch, she grabbed a trowel
and set to laying blocks.

Course after course she laid, till in through the doorway
she papered the hall, stairs and landing
—the cornice the tricky bit.

Then switching on the kettle as her kids turned in their sleep
the constellations swirling in the sky,
she sat in to the fire with the sage she'd clipped
from a neighbour's garden two doors down
—and watched it catch in the flames.

Children of the Reservation II: Eddie

In his green fatigues and belt of hand grenades
you'd forget Eddie is just a fledgling,
a squab in *SpongeBob* socks due home for *Birds Eye*
fish fingers and chips, for dinner at six.
Last we heard he'd gone off Reservation
—a glimmer flickering at the edge

out beyond the boundary hedge,
where he sits on the burned-out wreck of a Honda *Civic*
that once turned loops on The Green
before being redeemed by hogweed pushing through the floor,
a wren nesting in the panel of its door
and Eddie weaving a new pattern for the estate
from the common, from the bitter vetch,
from the fields of self-heal and nettle.

Water arcs from an overflow spout
traffic unwinds from a roundabout
the desire path follows its own vein

Back to Class

I've been reading from my sick bed all about the upper strata:
sedimentary rocks, oxblood knots turning in on themselves
and, right at the top, hoofprints and blowholes
surging from down below.

Yet I can't say what draws me back to class,
to orbit the polished corridors in my sensible shoes,
whirligigging on the chance of one of Saturn's moons
or simply that terrarium

—the tiny bubbles on the bell jar's curve,
the succulents twitching in the gravel
beneath the classroom fug—
and the teacher on his genuine leather uppers.

Outside the window, truth and obstinacy
between the hollow ways.

Savage Acres

On the edge of the estate a balloon drifts
over TVs abandoned in the grass

in three-stripe tracksuit I drop my football boots
and crouching down to the dead grey glass

curl my fingers around a breeze block
and just as I've seen on the album cover of *Glass Houses*

launch it into a screen
—there's no need to flee

it's not as if I've set alight the *Eurospar*
and pedalled up the hill to watch the sparks,

no vested interests have yet to look on this savage acre
where I shatter my reflection in the dark.

A Suburban Sunday

The Sunday Times crossword done, your man
swirling round the tables with issues
of *An Phoblacht* held up to his chest;
you'd buy one, leave it on the table
and later varnish over the fact.
I'd only eyes for orange *Fanta*,
your cold, black pint and that unicorn.
In our house, back home after the pub,
we never talked about hunger strikes.

No. 1: Quality Street

Stretching a flysheet between the hooks in the garden wall,
the washing line and the wishing well,

No. 1 sifted the sand into an empty tin of *Quality Street*,
worked it well into the earth, bedding the succulents in.

News of a sandstorm had come:
high pressure over Europe and a low front over the Atlantic
that blew the Sahara north

where it fell as quartz in great beads of rain
pearling onto the hatchbacks parked across the estate.

She poured a river of silver over the surface
and waited for the roots to take hold.

My Bravery was Restored

under the Sitka spruce, though some days it was eucalypt
growing in the wardrobe

where I set a place for the bears: polar, grizzly, Kodiak, or Yogi
who nonchalantly do-be-doo'd on through

while I sat playing out the distance of the two-second delay
down the line to my father, through fur coats

hung on branches, low-slung leather belts
and that tangle of children's sandals.

It's Wormed into Him from the Nest

this sense of living close together
of *come in out of that and sit down*
by the hearth where the anthracite glows.

Till bedtime and the dark of the stair,
the banister passed hand over hand,
he turns, traces back the night

and barefoot walks the garden in the rain.

Children of the Reservation III: Mykal

They'll always find a way home, pigeons
whose magneto-receptors distinguish their patch of pebbledash
from the hundreds of miles of pebbledash across the Reservation.

From just a few months old they learn to pick and peck,
get to know every speck and cinder block, every dandelion
in the yard, every dip and dimp in the walls that surround them.

Once upon a time, the pigeon loft was a fixture
in Belgium, like the *Spiegeltent* built by Oscar Mols Dom
whose name now adorns an Antwerp *Glaswerken*
'supplying glass doors and walls, bathroom glass
and splashbacks for your home'.

The Tent travelled to towns without dance halls
and has been on the road ever since.
During the Cabaret Show, Bath Boy
would trapeze and cavort high above the crowd
before diving to applause into the water.

Back on the Reservation,
Mykal sits beneath the corrugations
of her pigeon loft, staring into the future of flight:
soaring & tumbling, reaching new heights
high above the slate roofs,
and always finding her way home.

PART II

The Snib

This could be a poetry of domesticity
as neat and suburban as a garden gate's latch
dropped into place.

But the Difficulties are Glaring and Historical

Lines lifted verbatim from The Dublin Region: Advisory Regional Plan and Final Report Part I *(Government Publications, 1967).*

Hard choices have to be made; we cannot afford not to do so in this the motor age. Because one of the certainties of planning is that prosperity, once achieved, will spread.

There are of course disadvantages, especially for that half of the population who rely on public transport, who regard the walk to the railway station or bus, and the occasional wait in the rain, as part of the natural order of things. They will die of the cold believing it so.

We have in mind new housing in a favourable location, small industries, modernisation. The mountains and coasts of great beauty near which lie over a million people all dependent for their livelihood on the orderly guidance of regional growth.

A new pattern will be determined, and much of it will be constructed. Growth and change thereafter are certain. In brief, my colleagues and I have not 'planned' a population growth, but we will guide it.

Progress awaits.

Though drawbacks should be faced. This will call for some adjustment, though we have not sought to make such adjustments ourselves. The framework we propose can be supported by strong arguments, as far as our knowledge goes. Though the difficulties are at once glaring and historical.

There were doubts it would work.

The lip of a cup gasps for a coin
the clothes wilting on the line
the walkway to checkout No. 1.

Conversion: A Play in One Act

> *We felt the time was ripe for triple glazing,*
> *ran pitch pine to the ceiling*
> *and rag-rolled it all*
>
> *as you'll see above*
> *and below the dado railing*
> *made a lovely pair of cornice and skirting.*

No. 3 tongue 'n' grooves his colleagues
through the suburban woo of attic conversion

> *You can hang your woodchip wallpaper, gents,*
> *just not on my walls.*

Then the polish off
with the bottle of *Bend in the River*
glissfully poured
from glass to glass.

***

No. 3 dreams of Bayonne
        —Another Hine, Antoine—
of 45mpg in his blue *Megane*.

Down the hall his son places
rosewood bookends on the shelf.

From France he had asked them
for a plain *baton de pain;*

they brought him a snowstorm Tour Eiffel,
a frill of fol-de-dols from Les Halles,
a Moulin Rouge line about to kick …

*Mustn't wither, Son,
mustn't wither.*

***

Young Withers watches the knife sharpener
pedal up the street

sparks arcing across the road
as he heels the blade to the grindstone

*Mustn't wither, Son,
mustn't wither*

catches himself reflected in the tilted glass
of the cabinet filled with Samurai soldiers
all so lovingly moulded.

*They place, Son,
freshly picked flowers in their helmets,
good smell, you see,
for when they lose their heads.*

At the door the knife sharpener,
other side of the glass,
grinning at what young Withers
could never grasp.

The Camac gliding at high tide
the shopping trolley ripples down the aisle
the bottle of *Bend in the River*

The Housewives Sang and Hacked
at the Woodchip Walls

cracked the eggshell white,
then back through the first-born's baby blues
and on they hacked, their scrapers ringing true.

Through a thousand Saturdays of woodchip walls,
ten thousand mugs of tea,
to the distempered ground that was trampled down
by the dancing Ceile Dé
and down in the ground where the dead men go
to the maggot-feeding plagues.

Till ecstatically they tore at the new-marriage magnolia,
ripped sheets of woodchip up to the cornice
and, dusted down, screamed *Hallelujah!*
to raw cement and plaster.

Mary Dwyer, it was whispered,
did it in nothing but a shower cap
and *Sizzlers.*

From the Shoulder of Mutton Estate III

On warm days we'd place the television on the window ledge
    and move the house outdoors,
wheel out the *Superser* and make a table of it
    with a throw gifted by a neighbour;
the bottle of *Kosangas* was hooked up to the burner
    and we'd bubble a pot of stroganoff
while Jaime talked us through wild mushrooms and strips of beef
    cooked in a flash.
The kids were sent round the estate with bucket and spade
    in search of parsley
as the deckchairs we'd swapped for a card of SuperValu stamps
    were placed round the rockery
—the salt from a day at the beach
    drying on the hatchback's bonnet.
In the evening, we lit fairy lights round the wisteria
    as the crows settled in the plane trees
and in our navy flip-flops that came with every purchase
    of *Nivea Sun Cream*
—and thanks to satellite TV—we all settled in to watch
    Birds of a Feather.

Welcome, Oh Wheels!

a montage on housing

THE STATE SHALL CHERISH growth
    and tender envelopes
mohair, laughter, right living,
    Put her there!

AND BY ITS POSITIVE LAWS
    guide frugal comfort schemes
and where appropriate
    protect as best it may

HOMESTEADS WHICH PAY THEIR WAY.
    Old age, off plans.
Good name that: Setanta Phoenix
    & Sons.

THE STATE DESIRES that men
    should live in Great Beauty
ACCORDINGLY MAY AS OCCASION REQUIRES
    enact the orderly exercise of borrowing
borrowing borrowing

and UNDERTAKES NEVER TO DELIMIT
    the pursuit by law
of a Beautiful View:
    To render the people Moved.

And the Whole World is Adrift with Perfume

as I unbolt the door and lean to catch
an orange scarf
                    that, landing in the woods,
brings reasonable doubt to its knees.

It's there they find her
watching the woods from her room,

counting the stars hung between the trees;
the fallen, the flayed, the skeleton trees.

From the Upstairs Window She Blends the Twilight with an Oyster Knife

draws a storm of salt over the sole hung on the line,
and spots a young man hauled out of bed
and heeled aboard a fishing smack

that hoves out through an ordeal of shallows and shoals
bonefrail past the graving docks—the *zona desafectee*—
the hull heaving the roll, the after-whiskey ichthys
whuddering in his veins.

Against contrary winds they sail for days
bending for a tolerable anchorage,
past cavemouths, an overhang of karst and shale
where he dreams of mackerel-tailed women
spinning above the sails,

while she draws her brush over the old fish bones,
the candlelight stellate on the bay
all weight all washed away.
And closes the window oyster tight.

She Arcs Night Music from The Heights

blending old tunes with dark blues
she blows out the window
to where the knife sharpener
grinds a hard edge down
shooting sparks around the Avenue
as the kids come out to play
and burn their brown eyes blue.

The Line

The ringlets, if she had them,
would have bounced

but he'd unrolled them, teased them out
one by one

unfurled her hair

>   *once more,* she cried,
>   *once more, Daddy,*
>   *watch me fly*

and clear into the sky
as the father loosed his watch
to lift, then lay, the final building block

>   *once more,* she cried,
>   *once more, Daddy,*
>   *watch me fly*

and he laid the final block
then let slip the line

and from the lip of the sill
he too sailed clear
over Steeven's Hill

>   feeling young again
>   feeling flight again

>   *Daddy,* she cried, *Daddy watch me fly,*
>   and he watched it all
>   every leap, every splash, every fall.

We Made a Fist of It

Nobody said it would be easy
wringing water from a towel

or rendering a breach in the wall
with the deft flick of a trowel;

your knuckles catch on the pebbledash
which blooms gentian violet.

The Ordinariness of Living

with marble floors and her green eyes
brighter than the fire where she danced
absorbed by what she knew to be true:

that hands remember every fire they set,
lips recall every mouth they touch
and every fall of rain is a home from home.

Leaving the Estate

Wrapped in her duffel coat she stepped on the boat,
stood on the deck the whole way
then trundled down the gangplank where she fell in
with a group of angel-headed schoolchildren
marching Jungle-Booked together over the zebra crossing,
the arm of a yellow puffa held to a navy parka
that trailed the swallow-tail of a double-knit
hitched to the teacher who led them all across the road
—seven all told;
their feet dominoed down the streets
where she noticed there were no nettles
she could grasp and hold in the palm of her hand.
The seagulls kept up their euphonious senate.

A Child's Fare

If I were God I'd be the girl on the airport bus,
her mother keeping the driver distracted,
arguing the toss of a child's fare
while her daughter works the passengers.

The Apple Watch she slips from the wrist
of the man whose gaze she holds
reminding him that he was once a boy
who watched his mother cry.

You've seen me once to shed a tear and
let that be the end, my boy, now clean your plate
and go and wash your face don't leave the facecloth
lying on the floor.

The water stung, the soap just wouldn't sud,
he saw the jellied veins on his father's hands.
The water ran and he bared his teeth,
felt his pockets fill with sand,

felt the carpet curl beneath his feet,
the corners of the bathroom folding in,
the next-door neighbour's cat slip out—
and woke to a girl floating down the aisle
as if she walked on water.

I Love the Ether ... and All That Flies Up There

Gods never appear as seagulls, no matter the ferns
fretting the broken roof tiles in an orange-warning wind.

As time, that smells of my son climbing into bed beside me
these yawning mornings of November,

is silhouetted behind the thin, diminishing blinds of a neighbour
slippering to the clang of the church's belltongue,

the dried marrow of a rib snaffled from the BBQ place below
drops onto the ledge of my window.

And I reply with my best blue smile to the magpie on the railings
twitching to the chimes that wash over the rising tide

of roofs and reluctant lives wrestling from the skies
the mewling cries of seagulls.

The pull on the handle of a bag for life
a blister pack of pills
the turning point of a family gift
curling under the stairs.

No. 4

Lucy's work takes her as far as the garden shed—
she often stops to cut her fringe on the way out.

There is nowhere to sit in her shed
just a gas ring where Lucy fries button mushrooms.

On the way to work she picks up all the leaves
that have fallen from the apple tree,

pours them into a vat of clear glue she rolls into a sheet
and hangs on the line just to let the light shine through.

Those Pale Irretrievables

Is it for such I agitate my heart?

The asymptote of pram wheels
    through a powdering of snow,
the parallel bars of the gymnast
    in whites, vest to toe,
the garden pillars painted
    "SWEET DREAMS"   "ARE MADE OF THESE",
the canvas vanes of the windmill
    originally turning for show,
modified now to power the home.

The snap of a binder, the architrave
the afternoon of softening cornflakes
the coving, the glissade
the dip in the day.

I Could Haul a Rattle of Tools

from the amber-handled carpet bag—
a fireguard and poker, an awl, a push mower
and the scullery sink we always took when we moved.

The crack of static electricity brings the cat
that minces round the green flex of our 3-bar heater,
the timer on the blanket clicks into life
and snow seethes against the window.

The curl of an eyelash, the turn of a heel
the fury of ice on the windscreen
—cyclists in lycra steam by.

Children of the Reservation IV: Burney

If I were an ice-skater,
I'd perform the pigeon wing
over this glittering, frozen Green

where I lean to the side,
to crook the child on my hip,
showing everyday a little more wrist.

But it's my stare that's cold,
a feather's flick past care,
and soon this child will show.

Though maybe it'll be a pigeon-pair
who, with nothing but a bellyful of crumbs,
will flock, take flight and flee the estate.

The Verve on the radio the bus driver plays
the workers scull home at close of day
magpies whirl through the gloaming.

I Slide off the Rexine Sofa

and into a lagoon,
down through the water where the shopping trolleys lie.

Hand over hand I swim to the far shore
where she sits singing
and there we wait among the sand dunes

for the sunrise illuminations.

Streetlights loom over The Green
the whirl in the night of the washing machine
the belly of frost in the freezer.

The sway, the sashay, the missed spin class
legs of Pinot streaming the glass
the turn of your head
at the key in the door.

Collared Up Against the Evening's Kango Hammering

Past the concrete cracks and waves of corrugation,
I slip light along the pockmarked brick-in-the-wall.

Up steps the ganger, clips the Tonge & Taggart Foundry
cap with the handy end of a pick
and shifts his gaze to the wary dark below—
Oh Strangeways here we go.

The suburban organ music skeined in cables
I follow out to the coast,
and, to the humming aneurysm of information,
wade softly into the water.

ACKNOWLEDGEMENTS

With thanks to the Editors of the following print and online publications where versions of some of these poems appeared:

Banshee, The Cormorant, Isolation Poemcards (Dedalus Press), *Local Wonders,* ed. Pat Boran (Dedalus Press), *Migrant Shores: Irish, Moroccan & Galician Poetry,* ed. Manuela Palacios (Salmon Poetry), *Poetry Ireland Review, The Poetry Programme* RTÉ Radio 1, RTÉ Culture 'Poem of the Week', Strokestown Poetry Competition, *WRITE Where We Are Now* (Manchester Metropolitan University).

All lines from 'But the Difficulties are Glaring and Historical' (p. 42) are lifted verbatim from Myles Wright, *The Dublin Region: Advisory Regional Plan and Final Report Part I* (Government Publications, Stationary Office, Dublin, 1967).

Lines from 'Welcome, Oh Wheels!' (p. 49) are lifted verbatim from: Articles 40.3.2 and 43 of the Irish Constitution/ Bunreacht na hÉireann, from various Dáil Éireann / Houses of the Oireachtas debates, from Eamonn De Valera's 1943 St. Patrick's Day Radio Broadcast, and from various property and construction advertisements in the press.

'The Sound of Things to Come' – *Beauty is a rare thing: The Complete Atlantic Recordings,* Ornette Coleman (Rhino Records, 1993). *The Sound of Things to Come,* Various Artists, (CTI Records, 1977).

'Children of the Reservation III: Mykal' – lines taken from OMD Glaswerken, https://www.omd-glaswerken.be/

'The Housewives Sang and Hacked at the Woodchip Walls' – 'Down In The Ground Where The Dead Men Go,' The Pogues, *Red Roses for Me* (Stiff Records, 1984).

'Those Pale Irretrievables' – "Is it for such I agitate my heart?" Sylvia Plath, 'Elm,' *Ariel* (Faber and Faber, 1965).

'Collared Up Against the Evening's Kango Hammering' – 'Oh Strangeways here we go,' adapted from *Strangeways, Here We Come,* The Smiths (Rough Trade, 1987).

Untitled poems introduced by a ⏤ are taken from '36 Views from a Housing Estate' (after Hokusai).

With the greatest appreciation to the poet friends & readers whose time and expertise with this manuscript assisted in seeing me clear through to the Savage Acres: Mary O'Malley, Grace Wells, Theo Dorgan, Paula Meehan, Angela Long, Dean Browne, James Mc Naughton, Mary O'Donoghue and Su Garrido Pombo.

To those who accompanied me unawares through the making of this book, some of whose lines were savagely magpied for these acres.

To Pat Boran and Raffaela Tranchino of Dedalus Press, whose tireless graft in the forge keeps many poets alight and illuminates the ecosystem where we find ourselves at home. Unha aperta moi forte to ye both.

The epigraph is from 'The New Estate' by Ciaran Carson (from *The New Estate and Other Poems,* The Gallery Press, 1988), by kind permission.